GW01339242

9 005216 593 OXFAM

After a While

A Book of Poems & Paintings

by

TOM KERR

Designed by Joanna Martin

PUBLISHED IN 1992 BY TOM KERR
© TOM KERR 1992

ALL RIGHTS RESERVED. NO PART OF THIS PUBLICATION MAY BE REPRODUCED, STORED IN A RETRIEVAL SYSTEM, OR TRANSMITTED IN ANY FORM OR BY ANY MEANS, ELECTRONIC, MECHANICAL, PHOTOCOPYING, RECORDING OR OTHERWISE, WITHOUT THE PRIOR WRITTEN PERMISSION OF THE COPYRIGHT HOLDER.

BRITISH LIBRARY CATALOGUING IN PUBLICATION DATA

ISBN 0-9518316-1-5

AFTER A WHILE
A BOOK OF POEMS AND PAINTINGS BY TOM KERR.

THIS FIRST EDITION IS A LIMITED EDITION OF 2000 COPIES

PRINTED IN NORTHERN IRELAND BY
NICHOLSON & BASS LIMITED

For my children

Mamore Hill, Inishowen, Donegal

FOREWORD

Tom Kerr's art group which meets regularly in Holywood and at Ballygilbert is an important focal point for artists in the North Down area. On the occasions that I attended I soon came to realise the exceptional nature of this group.

For many years Tom has shared his experience and enthusiasm for watercolour painting, influencing those he meets, broadening their awareness of the subtleties of the medium. As someone who works predominantly in watercolour I am indebted to him for his dedication.

It is a delight to be associated with this second volume of poems and paintings, a welcome companion to his first.

Many thanks Tom for enriching our living.

Neil Shawcross.

NEIL SHAWCROSS

AFTER A WHILE   Tom Oct.91

The title of the book came to me first, and the words of the poem followed quickly afterwards. When I had written the poem, I remembered that the words occurred in a poem which my mother used to recite to us when we were children, 'Try Again', by Eliza Cook. It tells the well-known story of King Bruce and the spider:

> *"He flung himself down in low despair,*
> *As grieved as man could be;*
> *And after a while he pondered there,*
> *I'll give it all up, said he."*

However, inspired by the spider's repeated efforts, the king

> *"tried once more as he tried before,*
> *And that time did not fail."*

AFTER A WHILE

After a while will we travel again
the dark forgotten path
that brought us here before?
Will we know once more
a childhood's joy and pain,
or taste again,
in a strange new world, forbidden fruits?
Will we make our way
through half-known, dim-remembered thoughts,
walking the stony road,
close-bound by mortal day and night,
edging ever closer to the final light?

A CHILD

When stars are stilled,
and planet earth is dust;
when all along the streets of heaven,
like sifted sand for number,
saints and sinners dreadful stand,
perhaps we shall hear,
through the firmament clear,
gentle and mild,
the voice of a child,
tell us of the love we could have known;
tell us of the love we should have shown.

Johnny and Robbie

MY DREAMS

Tread gently on my dreams,
for now, after a lifetime,
it seems
that they more precious grow.
I cannot know
just how, or where my heart should go
in search of love.
And so,
wounded and hurt by harsh reality,
I sometimes hope and solace seek
in fields beyond eternity.

FIRST MAN

Are you the first man that was born?
Were you brought forth before the hills? Job 15.7

Did you exist when darkness dwelled,
When all was void and nothingness?
Could you have seen, with your own eyes,
dark waters move at His command,
and through the blackness of the skies
the amber light of that first dawn?
How came the mountains and the hills,
the torrents, lakes and rills?
Were you the man
who stepped into that wondrous glade?
Just how was your first journey made?

Old Friends

A January Morning

SNOWFALL

"There'll be snow before I'm very much older"
he said to his friend.
And sure enough, before they reached the end
of the street,
the first fine feathers were softly, silently,
drifting down.
An invading army determined to land and stay:
to conquor the drab, black earth
in a single hour, a single day:
to round the angles, sharp and harsh,
and paint them white.
And then at night, when the skies turned clear,
to mirror the light of the moon and stars,
and to frost the windows and roofs of cars.

WINTER WEARY

God grant me to know the warm, sweet days of spring again.
I am tired of the snow, the sleet and the rain.
Tired of winter, and all it brings,
the cold dark days, when no bird sings.
I long to sit at my back yard door,
to see once more
the sun climb higher and higher each day,
above the beeches across the way.
I want to feel this wintered earth
tremble and shake, and wake
to the hope of an April morn,
the wonder and glory of things new-born.

The primrose gleams with its pale yellow flower everywhere, but nowhere more sweetly than in the roadside ditches around Dunaff, Donegal.   Tom Nov. 91

SPRING IN DUNAFF

Michael's sheep have their lambs by their sides.
The cuckoo calls,
and the warm spring sun
glints on the rocks,
that hide in their shadows,
deep and dark,
the primrose, Spring's most lovely flower,
bright risen from its winter bed,
to greet the singing lark.

"Spring's most lovely flower"

DUNAFF, DONEGAL

The cloud cleared from Fanad,
and the lighthouse, like a slim white pencil,
shone in the morning sun.
Standing high on Mamore,
we watched, as one by one,
the distant peaks of Donegal stood clear,
pale, purple, grey,
and far below the patterned fields,
and cottages with brightly painted sills and doors,
and Lenan's soft curved bay.
Across the valley floor
the strong high headland shelters in its lee,
the little homes,
and to the west
it fights with barbed rocks
the ever sounding sea.

TIME GOES BY

I did not notice the second which has just gone by,
nor all the ones before,
although they made an hour or more.
I cannot make them pass me by again,
nor all my previous days, and weeks, and years.
Do they still hold within their hand,
in some strange limbo land,
capsules of laughter, pain, and tears?
What of this moment now?
Does it not have, in some way I can never see,
the very essence of eternity?

The Morning After the Snow

Seapark, Holywood

The summer of 91 produced several glorious sunsets. Walking along the shore at Seapark, people were stopping each other and commenting on the awesome beauty of the sky.   Tom Sept.91

THE SUNSET

They stop, and look, and say,
"Surely we do not deserve to know such wonders."
Can you pass by and not observe
the molten mantle of the sky,
the crimson bars,
pierced by a golden light,
the vapour trail of some giant flight.
And long before the blackness of the night
spreads dusky wings,
the author of it all,
the dipping, round, red sun,
holds us in thrall.
For now at last,
we stand in awe.
A tiny breath,
and glory's diadem is past.

TOWARD EVENING ON A FINE SUMMER DAY

I know no better time
than when, at daylight's end,
the long wave curves along the shore,
voices grow silent,
and the edge of heaven skirts the western sky.
For then it seems the whole world round
is bathed in peace.
Sorrows softer lie on sorrow's bed,
and old men know, for those who wait and weep,
a brighter day will dawn,
a day when hearts will sing,
and troubles will be fled

On the Evening Tide

Calm Waters

Everyone who has watched the red-sailed yachts coming ashore at the end of the day at Cultra, must be aware of the sights and sounds mentioned in this poem. Tom Aug.91

CULTRA EVENING

The sun grows tired of his strength at last,
and reddens away to the west.
The day's fresh breeze drops cool and calm,
and sails lie limp against the mast.
Voices echo across the sea,
as one by one the boats sail in,
and are rumbling, grumbling, pulled ashore.
The folk who watch from the battery wall,
who have seen this many times before,
marvel and sigh at the sunset sky,
call their dogs to heel, and turn for home.

THE FORGOTTEN GARDEN

I will take you to that secret place
where wonder dwells,
all magic, green, translucent dwells.
We'll walk, we two alone,
by sapphire streams,
and far above a bright new sun will shine.
Sweet music will with gentle airs combine
to clothe our days with happiness.

At golden dawn or twilight's end
(What memory this?)
we'll hear His voice,
and know we have a friend.

The people who lived in all the little terraced streets of Belfast formed a tightly knit community, and knew a great deal about the true meaning of the word "neighbours".   Tom Feb.92

THE BACK STREETS OF BELFAST

*T*hey had a way with them,
the folk who lived in all those little streets.
They scrubbed their steps,
and leaned against their brick door jambs
to pass the time of day
with neighbours who had done the same
just across the way.
It seemed a shame,
when faceless men decided that the time had come
to build each one "a better home".

Their terraces were brought to dust like packs of cards.
The cobbled streets were gouged and torn,
and all too few were left to mourn
the passing of their way of life.

And now the grand new roads that skirt the water's edge,
and carry endless lines of cars,
rest on the setts and bricks of countless homes,
on humble papered walls
that formed the bedrooms, kitchens, yards and halls,
and steps that children's children bore,
which now are scrubbed no more.

The Last Lamp

WAITING

A chill wind was blowing,
and the rooks were noisy in the winter trees,
when I saw him, with hope-bright eyes,
waiting, his arm along the gate.

And I saw her, slow stepped, unseen by him,
hesitate,
then turn and slip away.

The last light rays were fading when I passed again,
and saw him waiting still,
in vain...in vain.

In after years, for good or ill,
when'er the wind is blowing chill,
and rooks are noisy in the trees,
he will remember how he waited there,
when winter's light was dim,
and how, in spite of promise made,
she never came to him.

CHOICE

What mystery this,
that I, at any time, a choice can make,
by day or night.
And I can take or leave
a thought or hope which might my future weave.
What gentle power can alter my command,
and stay my rash impulsive hand?
Does someone sit beside the placid sea
and say to me,
when I have fished all day to no avail,
"Let me decide,
just cast your nets upon the other side."

I am often asked to do a "painting of Holywood", and when I ask what the subject of such a painting should be, the usual answer is "The Old Priory".   Tom Dec.91

THE OLD PRIORY, HOLYWOOD

Did men dictate the way each stone was laid,
or did a hand mysterious play its part,
to give us such a gentle ruin,
which, by whatever light, can tug our heart?
You ancient stones, all clustered round
with memories of former days,
what can you say to those who now pass by,
with selfish thought, and cold uncaring eye?

Long past the nidnight hour, when stars look down,
do you, calm, watch us all,
the dead and living of this town?

The Old Priory, Holywood

THE MIRACLE

There is a lad here who has five barley loaves and two fish. John 6,9

Not fishes twain, nor barley baps,
but tons we have of fodder.
And still we cannot find a way
to share with one-anodder.

WELL?

"Grandad, are you very old?"
"I'm pretty old" I said.
"Grandad, "Do you sometimes think
that you might soon be dead?"

POWER

The BMW climbed the hill,
with never a sign of cough or ill.
The driver inside could sit and talk;
he didn't think to get out and walk.

PLEASURES

Roses as sweetly grow
in my neglected plot,
as in the grandest gardens anywhere.
And there is not
a finer blackbird in the air,
than he who daily sings for me,
from my uncared for apple tree.
The same blue sky
rewards my eye
as that which pleases kings and queens.
And no-one knows
a brighter moon or sun
than those which shine on me.
So why should I not joyful be,
and sing for very ecstasy!

THE BIRDS

All of a sudden
out of the icy sky
the starlings came.
Shiny and sharp,
with hungry eye,
swooping on scraps
that earlier I
had spread beneath the apple tree.
The jacks, and rooks, and hooded crow
came darker down,
and, swaying, sat above the snow;
timid, although
they bigger, stronger were.
A blackbird and a robin came
to join the starlings on the ground,
and then the sky was filled with sound
as all around the birds flew in.

The sleek black tom was furtive, sly,
with mayhem gleaming in his eye.
He in his turn, just failed to see,
his crouching form was watched by me..

"Out of the icy sky"

Earth, so the astronomers tell us, is the only planet in the solar system which experiences in certain places, at certain times, a total eclipse of the sun.   Tom Feb.92

THE SUN'S ECLIPSE

Pale moon,
all barren dust and stones,
do you in envy view
this gleaming blue-veined ball,
bright gem in velvet black,
held in your eternal stare?
Are you aware
of all the frenzied race
that ebbs and flows beneath your
cold unchanging face?

But you must know,
when cosmic laws ordain it,
you stand, for one brief jot,
in space and time,
exactly so,
that with your lifeless sphere
you blot from view,
the very source of light, and heat, and power,
from myriad,
wondering mortals here.

THE EXPANDING UNIVERSE

*F*olk who know,
say the stars I see
in the sky at night, quite possibly,
have ceased to be.
The Milky Way, and the Little Bear
are no longer there.
They departed a million years ago,
and so - just think,
it could very well be,
that someone, somewhere, wherever it may be,
thinks the very same thing
about you and me.

The Turf Bog

After the Storm

THE SPACE PROBE

Frail object,
made and sent by man,
to seek and know
new worlds, new spheres,
where we can never go.
Tell us, as you pass them by,
and gaze with your computered eye,
just how the planets move around our sun.
Do you enjoy it all,
and find some fun
in Saturn's rings,
in tawny Mars, or Venus bright,
and do you care a single jot
for mighty Jupiter's red spot?

And then at last,
when all we know has ceased to be,
spread your diaphanous wings
and journey on past time and space.
Perhaps, with us,
you'll see His face.

THE TRINKET

He often spoke of his boyhood days,
his holidays by the sea,
wandering under the wheeling sky,
alone and dreaming - free.
Few were told of the gentle girl,
in the bright print dress, on the shining sand;
of the tiny bauble she gave him there,
while walking together, hand in hand.
For he was a lad on a morning shore,
and he vowed to keep it for evermore.

They tidied away his potions and pills,
from the cupboard beside his bed.
No need now to keep these things,
now that he is dead.
Why on earth did he want to keep
this little trinket...tawdry, cheap,
wrapped in tissue, so carefully,
from the town he loved beside the sea?

FOOTSTEPS

The sky changed from blue to grey,
from white to gold to red,
each day,
each hour.
And yet each day my path remained unchanged.
Each footstep where a former footstep lay,
on rock,
on grass,
on sand.
Only on sand until the searching tide
could brush the marks aside,
saying as each ripple swelled and died,
"Come back another day."
"Come back another day."
"And do not grieve or mourn
the solitary marks just made by you.
I too remember former times
when they were made by two."

Footsteps

THE SHIPYARD

To the yard,
where the great ships were being built
for peace and war,
we came, his sons,
to tell him of his brother's death.
I remember how he came down to us,
standing by the vast grey flank,
and all around the iron noise.
Three tiny specks
among ten thousand men.
He in his work-stained clothes,
with work-stained hands,
hearing the news with low-bowed head.

Now on the ocean bed
that ship is rusting fast.
He and those who worked with him
as often is the way of things,
themselves lie long since dead.

A GREY DAY

Monotonous and grey,
that February day:
grey chimneys against a grey sky,
grey people passing by
my window.
And I, confined to bed,
half wishing I were dead,
felt just as grey as they:
but realised there was a corner of my room
wherein there was no gloom,
just golden light!

A bunch of daffodils,
surely a sight
that presaged brighter days,
blue skies and sunshine,
soft airs,
the skylark's praise!

The Bridle Path

Outside the Cottage

I suppose everyone, at some time in their lives, has had a fleeting glimpse of heaven; just as I suppose everyone, sadly, has also had a fleeting glimpse of hell.   Tom April92

A GLIMPSE

Something happened,
and for one frail, fragile moment,
he saw and knew.
He saw the veil withdrawn,
the dark endeavour fled,
and in the lucent light,
he, and everything around, shone white, all white.
And he could touch and feel the gleaming air,
like any silken tress.
The second passed, but still the wonder dwelled,
for he had known, in truth,
the very breath of holiness.

AN ANGEL'S SONG

No sound.

No sound in the moss-damp wood.

Only the ceaseless drip from barren autumn twigs

in the chill November mist.

And then I heard a voice,

softly at first,

a song so sweet,

such as an angel sings.

The whole wood came alive and shone for me,

as if by some strange alchemy.

I had to see!

I struggled through the briars,

my hands were torn.

(Do angels sing to us before our souls are born?)

I stopped to listen by an ancient tree.

Only the chill November mist enfolded me.

Fishing - no better sport

The Picnic

THE ARTIST

I have no palette to paint the sky,
when the winter geese are flying high
against the twilight moon.

I have no palette to paint the land,
when the earth is black in the digger's hand
on the bleak turf bog at noon.

I have no palette to paint the sea,
when the waves run white and the sea-birds flee
shrieking before the gloom.

I have no palette to paint your brow,
when your eyes are cold, and I ask you how
you can say farewell so soon.

ROBIN

The redbreast kept me company
in stuttered flight,
from post to post,
down the steep path
through frosted air,
watching me with lively eye;
together he and I.
Strange pair!
He left me at the copse's edge,
flying to cold winter's dome.
So I missed my little friend.
Alone, and sad, I wandered home.

Young Girl

Lake District Sheep

THE JOURNEY

Where you go I will go. Ruth 1,16

How can I go where you have gone?
Can I make my way through the shining stars
to touch your hand,
past angels' wings to hear your voice?
Will not the fiercely glowing light beyond the skies
be all too bright for my earth eyes?

Thus is all my yearning vain,
or will the pain itself, at last,
make clear the path between us,
and help to hold me fast?

REMEMBER ME

Last night I heard the seagulls cry,
and the curlews call
to the darkening sky.
I heard the storm through the leafless trees,
black as the clouds against the moon.
And far away I heard the sea,
and a voice that said
"Remember me."

The morning wakened, calm, serene,
the eastern sky
all golden light.
I heard a blackbird hail the dawn,
and clear between his notes long-drawn,
still far away I heard the sea,
and the voice that said
"Remember me."

Towards the Gap

The Back of the Hill

THE PHOTOGRAPH ALBUM

Here it is,
the photograph I took of you on holiday.
I remember every detail now:
the rock on which you stood along the shore,
the pale blue dress, the cardigan you wore,
your watch, your shoes, your wedding ring,
your smile.
So you have stayed forever young,
while years have marked my brow.

I sit beside the fire, the embers dead.
The photograph is blurred. I cannot see.
Only wistful memories stab at me.

SOJOURNERS

No-one can tell us how we ought to travel,
or how we should unravel
the tightly woven web
that girds our waking (and our sleeping) ways.
We long to break the bonds,
to walk the high hill path,
find freedom in the silver air,
but still we stand afraid.
For looking back,
we see spread out,
the errors we have made.

THE LAST PAGE OF THE BOOK

Do you, like me,
remember those far distant days?
Did you know then we trod another world,
and did you realise,
that quite unknown to us
a tiny part of life's sad tale was being played?
Would you have stepped aside,
if you had been allowed to look,
to read the final pages of the book?
Like others we could only journey on,
for hope, like love, our life transcends,
and no-one knows just how the story ends.